# Bull-Shiht

## Designer Dogs Gone Barking Mad

# Bull-Shiht

## Designer Dogs Gone Barking Mad

### Frank N. Stein

Saraband

This book is meant to be absurd. Dogs should be treated with respect and not as our playthings or designer accessories. Don't get a dog unless you are willing to make the commitment to look after it properly.

Acknowledgments
Dr. Frank N. Stein was aided by the contributions of Donna Freed and Sara Hunt.

Dog photography © Nikki L. Fesak; all other images © 2006 Jupiterimages.

Bull-Shiht artists: Fiona Fox, Deborah Hayes & Sara Hunt.

Thanks are also due to Heidi Helm and Simon Saunders.

Published by Saraband (Scotland) Ltd.
The Arthouse, 752–756 Argyle Street,
Glasgow, G3 8UJ, Scotland
hermes@saraband.net
www.saraband.net

Copyright © 2006 Saraband (Scotland) Ltd.

ISBN 13: 978-1-887354-47-9
ISBN 10: 1-887354-47-6

Printed in China

1 2 3 4 5   10 09 08 07 06

# CONTENTS

# INTRODUCTION

If you can have a mocha soy decaf latte with a twist instead of a regular cup of joe, why not design everything in your life to be just the way you like it? Labradoodles and Cockapoos are *so* last year, so it's time to customize your very own canine. We hope that our unique characters will inspire you, but remember: JUST BE CAREFUL WHAT YOU WISH FOR!

# WORKING DOGS

**B**eing man's best friend is one thing, but earning your keep is quite another. If you're looking for a dog that will be your helpmate as much as your soulmate, but haven't found the one that suits your precise requirements, the following pages might inspire you to think a little more creatively about canine potential.

# West Winger

## West Highland terrier

Charismatic
Popular

Temperament: Diplomatic
Grooming needs: Full-time staff
Exercise needs: Jogging, cycling, gym
Obedience: Responsive, but scheming
Ideal Owners: Presidential candidates

## Springer spaniel

Clever
Duplicitous
Persistent

**Why You Should**
You'll win

Okay so you've won the nomination--congratulations. Now the hard part: picking your presidential pooch! You need a smart, personable, good-looking fellow, sweet enough to swing votes from the most solid states, yet savvy enough to sniff out hidden enemies, and smart enough to outwit them. Soon you can let him take over so you can focus on fundraising for his reelection campaign.

**Why You Shouldn't**
His "Doggygate" problem

# Soberman

**Doberman pinscher**
Insane
Athletic
Hyperactive

Temperament: Just plain dangerous
Grooming needs: He's completely clean
Exercise needs: Lunges and thrusts
Obedience: Military-style discipline
Ideal Owners: Reforming alcoholics

**Staffordshire bull terrier**
Loyal & devoted
Vicious

This is the perfect gift for someone who is serious about cleaning up his act: the Soberman will police the post–New Year's-resolution, non-drinking, nonsmoking regime. A righteous character, he will keep his owner on the straight and narrow when he might be tempted back to his old habits. No need to put a lock on the drinks cabinet.

Why You Should
You know you need to

Why You Shouldn't
Can you handle him?

# Boston Strangler

**Boston terrier**
Lean
Mean
Dangerous

Temperament: High-strung
Grooming needs: Don't touch!
Exercise needs: Midnight flits
Obedience: Needs daily drills
Ideal Owners: Lonely criminals

**Spaniel/ Rottweiler**
A) Crazy
B) Savage

**Why You Should**
You need a sidekick

Even criminals feel the need for a furry friend. A Boston strangler can provide cover for those pesky restraining orders: "I was just walking my dog, Officer!" And if foolish people upset the strangler, he'll go to work rearranging their features and ensuring they won't be able to appear in the witness box.

**Why You Shouldn't**
His cut of the loot

# Bordellö

**Border terrier**

Aggressive
Lots of stamina
Sturdy

Temperament: Streetwise; good watchdog
Grooming needs: Flea powder/cheap scent
Exercise needs: Occasional chases
Obedience: Just show him the whips
Ideal Owners: Brothel owners; repo men

**Löwchen**

Playful
Flirtatious
Sassy

What every madame needs is someone to keep the johns in line while not scaring them off the premises before their pockets have been emptied. The Border terrier genes are perfect for keeping the punters under control while they're waiting for the girls, while the Löwchen instincts will make him steal their pants if they try to run off without paying.

**Why You Should**
He's cheaper than you are

**Why You Shouldn't**
Unsightly fur on your couches

# Spankit

**Spaniel**
Trainable
Loyal
Long-suffering

Temperament: Submissive
Grooming needs: He grooms you
Exercise needs: He's too tired
Obedience: Perfect
Ideal Owners: Disciplinarians

**Whippet**
Skinny
Underfed
Hardworking

**Why You Should**
You're needy

Are you a retired schoolmarm or nun, missing your paddle and ruler? Hopefully you're softening to some degree in your old age, but I'm sure that with your now-obsolete talents, you can still train the Spankit to use the toilet and clean up after itself. Don't be too hard on him, though, because he's doing his very best to please you.

**Why You Shouldn't**
You're in detention

**Anatolian shepherd**
Robust
Uncomplaining
Big

# Antifreeze

Temperament: Chilled
Grooming needs: Cold showers
Exercise needs: Bracing runs
Obedience: Rigid
Ideal Owners: Arctic-dwellers

**Bichon Frise**
Fluffy
Cuddlesome
Warm

Those of you in the Lower 48 wouldn't understand the need for the Antifreeze, but you could learn a thing or two from Alaskans. You might think their dog of choice is the Husky, for the Iditarods, but the real McCoy is the Antifreeze, combining the Bichon fluff for warmth with the stalwartness of the Anatolian Shepherd. You'll want at least nine of them to make a good blanket.

**Why You Shouldn't**
He'll eat your seal blubber

**Why You Should**
You're freezing

# Lab Coat

**Labrador**
Intelligent
Personable
Diligent

Temperament: Efficient
Grooming needs: Scrubs up well
Exercise needs: Circuits
Obedience: Perfect
Ideal Owners: Surgeons, dentists

**Smooth-coated collie**
Competent
Clever

**Why You Should**
You'll look smarter

Doctors have gotten a bad rap in recent years, what with leaving the sponge and scissors inside and removing the one good kidney, so they need a better image. What better to make a doc more friendly than having a dog, and who better than the Lab Coat? She's cool, calm and professional, and with those big brown eyes, she has bedside manner in spades.

**Why You Shouldn't**
She might replace you

# Cock & Bull

**Cocker spaniel**

Well-mannered
Persuasive
Faithful

Temperament: Charming, seductive
Grooming needs: Copious after shave
Exercise needs: Tailing punters
Obedience: If you pay him enough
Ideal Owners: Used-car salesmen

**Bulldog**

Diligent
Stubborn
Ugly

If you're selling, the Cock & Bull can help get them buying with a little bit of that old "good dog, bad dog" action. Just remember, while you may be the good-looking one, he's the good one, meant to make you appear less sleazy. His job is to be ugly on the outside and pretty on the inside, unlike you.

Why You Should
He's a great closer

Why You Shouldn't
Never trust a partner

## Dalmatian

Lightning fast
Fizzing
Telepathic

# Damnation

Temperament: Smouldering
Grooming needs: Purification by fire
Exercise needs: Chasing styx
Obedience: Needs a firm hand
Ideal Owners: Firemen

## Norwegian elkhound

Strong
Hunky

**Why You Should**

Fire prevention

Everyone knows that the energetic (some might say "tightly wound") Dalmatian loves a good fire and enjoys running with the trucks. Add in a few "Dog of the Vikings" genes, and the Damnation will go one step beyond.

**Why You Shouldn't**

Say your prayers

With its uncanny sixth sense, it hunts down firestarters, detecting a blaze before it's even lit. Just make sure you don't let him cross to the dark side.

**Anatolian
shepherd**
Intimidating
Moody
Confrontational

Temperament: Unhelpful
Grooming needs: DON'T touch her ears
Exercise needs: Anger-management class
Obedience: Don't go there
Ideal Owners: Customer service reps

**Samoyed**
Bad-tempered
Stubborn
Willful

Annoyéd? You would be too, if people couldn't pronounce
your name. The last syllable rhymes with "dead"--like
you'll be soon if you don't make
nice. This dog was bred for cus-
tomer-service telephone work, and
his forte is getting rid of the most persistent of
irate customers. Nothing, I mean nothing, gets rid
of unwanted callers faster.

Why You
Should
You've tried
everything else

Why You
Shouldn't
Where to
start?

# SPORTING & HERDING DOGS

OK, so unless you're Old Mother Hubbard, it's not strictly necessary to have a herder at home, but your pet could be useful in other ways: rounding up some companions when you're in the bar, for example. Read on!

**Bouvier des Flandres**

Thirsty

Thick-skinned

# Boozer

Temperament: Convivial
Grooming needs: Breath freshener
Exercise needs: Strolls between bars
Obedience: Very docile
Ideal Owners: Drinkers

**Schnauzer**

Rough

Vocal

Easygoing

**Why You Should**

You've got no friends

If you eschew the twelve little steps to sobriety and reason, you'd enjoy the company of a Boozer. He's very trainable: he can reach into your pocket for the money and balance the drinks on his head. He's imposing-looking but friendly, so you might not get 86ed as quickly with him as without him. And unlike you, he can actually carry a karaoke tune.

**Why You Shouldn't**

His Elvis impersonation

# Harry Porter

**Harrier**
Fast
20/20 vision
Efficient

Temperament: Ethereal
Grooming needs: Broomstick
Exercise needs: Chasing demons
Obedience: Out of this world
Ideal Owners: Magicians

**Portuguese water dog**
Ingenious
Has webbed feet

We all need a little magic in our lives, and if you're a neophyte white witch or wizard, there's no more useful accessory than the cuddliest, cleverest animal familiar: the Harry Porter. He doesn't need to be named Fluffy to detect demons and hunt them down. He's a great help with the chores and he'll make light work of your bags.

**Why You Should**
He's magic

**Why You Shouldn't**
You're not qualified

# Chowder

### Chow chow
Distinguished
Fluffy
Blue-tongued

### Border collie
Intelligent
Energetic
Independent

Temperament: Who cares? He's outside
Grooming needs: Agrochemicals
Exercise needs: That's his business
Obedience: Ask the sheep
Ideal Owners: Foodies with real estate

**Why You Should**
You're a fashionable weekend farmer

This is a good dog for someone who wants a herder that complements his flock of sheep and the white picket fences. The gourmet Chowder will look perfect while you're enjoying your champagne picnic on the neighboring hillock. Just make sure the property manager has cleaned up the sheep turds. You don't want your picnics ruined by nature.

**Why You Shouldn't**
Your seafood intolerance

# Sharp Point

**Shar-Pei**
Wrinkly
Likes creature
comforts

Temperament: Competitive
Grooming needs: Luxury spas
Exercise needs: Carrying the shopping
Obedience: Good if bribed
Ideal Owners: Wealthy fashionistas

**Pointer**
Fast
Focused
Can-do

You can hold your facelift high when people say you look like your dog, since you're less wrinkled than he is. Another bonus for the fashionista is that he has a real nose for fashion; he can sniff out a Barney's sale bargain at forty paces and get you to that Dolce & Gabbana shift dress as fast as your Jimmy Choos will take you.

**Why You Should**
You want a personal shopper

**Why You Shouldn't**
He's not pretty

# Sudoku

**Saluki**
Smart
Supercilious
Brilliant

Temperament: Platonic
Grooming needs: Tidy
Exercise needs: Mental challenges
Obedience: Socratic
Ideal Owners: Accountants, puzzlers

**Doberman pinscher**
Alert
Persistent
Disciplined

**Why You Should**
You want to win puzzle prizes

Deceptively simple and maddeningly addictive, Sudoku has eclipsed the verbose crossword. If you're a little intimidated and need help, get the canine puzzle master, the Sudoku. The brainy Saluki with a dash of disciplinarian Doberman provides the mental muscle to work the numbers while you relax with the Sunday newspaper.

**Why You Shouldn't**
She'll show you up

# Bedbug

### Bedlington terrier
Fluffy
Docile
Cuddly

Temperament: Snoozy
Grooming needs: Dry clean only
Exercise needs: Pillow laps
Obedience: Good when awake
Ideal Owners: Convalescents

### Pug
Tiny
Agreeable
Loving

So: you're confined to your bed for the foreseeable after a skiing accident in the Swiss Alps. Bed rest! What you need now is a friendly companion to curl up with you, fetch the bonbons, and peel your grapes, but not fight you for the remote. Order up a Bedbug, affectionate and cute. And unlike the purebred pug, she won't snore or wheeze.

**Why You Should**
You're lonely (sob)

**Why You Shouldn't**
She'll get the attention

# New Yorkie

**Newfoundland**
Big
Huge
Gigantic

Temperament: Brash
Grooming needs: Body wave
Exercise needs: Taxi!
Obedience: Yo--you talking to *me*?
Ideal Owners: Hipsters

**Yorkshire terrier**
Tiny
Selfish
Loud

Why You Should
It beats a T-shirt

New York, New York, it's a helluva town, so nice they named it twice. One thing that you can say about New York is that it is unique, and so is the New Yorkie. Just like its namesake, it's got attitude, and it's noisy, hairy, busy, bulky and slobbering; but you gotta love it anyway! (Or just deal with it and don't give it a reason to kill you.)

Why You Shouldn't
He's a panhandler

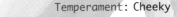

# Affable

**Affenpinscher**
Apelike
Amenable
Oddball

Temperament: Cheeky
Grooming needs: They clean each other
Exercise needs: Swinging on trees
Obedience: Yeah, why not?
Ideal Owners: Zoo keepers

**Bulldog**
Genial
Affectionate
Laid back

With a face only a mother could love, you better have a good personality. Affenpinschers ("monkey terriers") are, luckily, adorable, easygoing companions. Combined with a bit of bull, Bubba won't win any beauty contests, but you'll never want for someone to shoot the breeze with, especially if you're into hanging out in trees.

**Why You Should**
He'll be your buddy

**Why You Shouldn't**
If you can't take a joke

# Spandex

**Sussex spaniel**
Vain
Obsessive
Compulsive

Temperament: Prima donna
Grooming needs: Exorbitant salons
Exercise needs: Personal trainers
Obedience: She expects it from you
Ideal Owners: Anyone with a complex

**Dachshund**
Self-centered
Long
Lean

**Why You Should**
Need you ask?

Meet the Spandex, the latest must-have celebs' copycat accessory. Yoga junkies, join the line (sorry, there's no guest list!). The distinctive sausage

**Why You Shouldn't**
He'll outlive the fashion

shape is perfect for rolling neatly into your mat while enjoying an après-yoga soy latte, and the silky beast is allergic to everything but herself--so she's organic. All. The. Way. Got that?

# NON-SPORTING DOGS

Some dogs are, frankly, much too hyper, with daily exercise requirements that are too taxing for the not-so-sporty prospective owner. If you're not the type to go jogging every morning before breakfast,  perhaps you should look for a canine companion that will keep you company in a more low-maintenance, relaxing manner.

# Afghan Rug

**Afghan hound**

Sensitive
High-strung
Luxuriant

Temperament: Laid back
Grooming needs: Professional cleaning
Exercise needs: Nil
Obedience: Unquestioning
Ideal Owners: Hippies

**Pug**

Affectionate
Wrinkled
Diminutive

The road trip dog. Get your kicks on Highway 66 with your Afghan rug on your lap. He makes a wonderful companion: he's less skittish and prone to carsickness than the full-blood Afghan. Don't expect a lot of intellect: his specialty is long, comforting silences (OK, so he wheezes and snores, but you'll soon tune that out.)

**Why You Should** Fits in your glovebox

**Why You Shouldn't** Your RV has velour seats

53

# Shihtweiler

**Shih Tzu**
Indolent
Greedy
Vain

Temperament: Moody, but harmless
Grooming needs: *You cannot be serious?*
Exercise needs: Refrigerator to sofa
Obedience: AAA (against all authority)
Ideal Owners: Teenagers

**Rottweiler**
Has tantrums
Grows 24/7
Scary

Why You
Should
It's a
hormonal thing

You might not be able to tell the difference between your Shihtweiler and your teenager, as they're both loafing on the sofa watching TV, consuming all your food, staying up all night and snoring all day. It is important to lay down one ground

Why You
Shouldn't
It's a
hormonal thing

rule: make Shiht-for-Brains the Elder take Shiht-for-Brains the Younger for his walks, leaving you plenty of time to tidy up and make more food.

# Great Scot!

**Great Dane**
Viking
Proud
Knobbly-kneed

Temperament: Shaken, not stirred
Grooming needs: Curling
Exercise needs: Caber chasing
Obedience: See you, Jimmy
Ideal Owners: Campbells & McTavishes

**Scottie**
Tartan
Tightwad
Unintelligible

If you're into the haggis, single malts, the bagpipes, the tam o' shanter and the knobbly-knee-revealing kilt, why not celebrate your love of all things Scots in a big way, a VERY BIG way. Your love is vast, as deep as Loch Ness, so a wee Scottie is not enough. Beef him up to Braveheart size. But beware, if you're cheap like your Scottish granny, this dog can eat for all Scotland.

**Why You Should**
For auld lang syne

**Why You Shouldn't**
He's into Trainspotting

# Dorkie

**Doberman pinscher**
Dedicated
Boring
Uncool

Temperament: Nerdy
Grooming needs: Hates bathing
Exercise needs: Surfing (the net)
Obedience: Compliant
Ideal Owners: Nerds, dorks

**Yorkshire terrier**
Socially inept
Yappy
Irritating

**Why You Should**
He'll distract people from you

If you're not afraid to show your bookish side, and your glasses are thicker than the soles of your shoes, get yourself a Dorkie. Not only does he provide companionship, he looks smart enough to get into the library with you (if only to chew). And if anyone—*anyone*—tries to scatter your armload of books, the Doberman in him will be sure to make your attacker regret his foolish pranks.

**Why You Shouldn't**
He's a dorkie

# Balderdash

**Chinese crested bald**
Hairless
(Well, almost)

Temperament: Nonsensical
Grooming needs: Sponge bath
Exercise needs: He won't go out
Obedience: Submissive
Ideal Owners: Midlifers in crisis

**Dachshund**
Sausagelike
Lackluster
Thin-coated

"I'm not entirely bald," you think to yourself, wishfully. Neither is the Balderdash! And if anyone tells you other-wise--balderdash and hogwash to them! Guys, now that the combover's imminent and you're shopping for convertibles, what will REALLY get the ladies going is the Balderdash. Like you, he's thinning, but you can't be as ugly as him.

Why You Shouldn't
He is ridiculous

Why You Should
Your combover

# Old English Stiff

**Old English sheepdog**
Old
English

Temperament: Stiff upper lip
Grooming needs: Stiff brush
Exercise needs: Pub crawls
Obedience: What ho!
Ideal Owners: Old English stiffs

**Mastiff**
Stuck up
Repressed
Turgid

**Why You Should**
Two's company

Our Fido was born with a silver bone in his mouth, but he often seems jolly glum. After a few pints in the local pub, though, he'll soon cheer up. He specializes in losing at sporting contests of all kinds, but acquitting himself rather spiffingly in the process, because he's a plucky little chap at heart--though you wouldn't know it under that olde English reserve of his.

**Why You Shouldn't**
Life's too short

# Porker

**Portuguese water dog**
Rotund
Hearty
Hungry

Temperament: Stodgy
Grooming needs: Grease bath
Exercise needs: Fat chance
Obedience: Fat chance
Ideal Owners: Chubbies

**Cocker spaniel**
Indolent
Indulgent
Greedy

Pick up a Porker so as not to be shown up by a more slender pooch. Are you serious about tackling your diabetes? Train your Porker to catch fish, which you should be eating more of, instead of doughnuts. Like you, when he's bored, this dog will start to chew on anything handy, so be ready for lots of exercise to save your belongings.

**Why You Should**
Less is more

**Why You Shouldn't**
Too much temptation

## Samoyed
Clean
White
Decorative

# Smug

Temperament: Smug
Grooming needs: Eyelash curlers
Exercise needs: Abs 'n thighs video
Obedience: Stepford wife
Ideal Owners: Smug people

## Pug
Compact
Undemanding
Gift-wrapped

**Why You Should**
You haven't got one

What to get for the woman who has everything? There's not another inch of her body that she can drape in diamonds, there's not another inch of her body that can be nipped or tucked, and there's no inch of the spa-covered earth that she hasn't traveled (first class, of course). so it's time for the Smug. We can personally guarantee that no one else has one!

**Why You Shouldn't**
You'll get bored (yawn)

# French Dandie

**French bulldog**
*So* muscular!
*So* toned
Coordinated

Temperament: Dandy
Grooming needs: Boutonniere & cravat
Exercise needs: Dancing cheek to cheek
Obedience: Conditioned
Ideal Owners: Village people

**Dandie Dinmont**
Refined
Houseproud
Continental

Let's say you're a man and you have what your mother calls a "roommate" and you live in Greenwich Village. You were meant to be born in another age--the age of the top hat and cane, the age of wit and cocktails. What you need is a foil, but Shih Tzus are *so* yesterday. Go for the elegant, haughty, naughty French Dandie. You'll be talk of the town, darling!

Why You Should
You simply must!

Why You Shouldn't
He's too fragrant

## Jack Spaniel

**Jack Russell terrier**
Small
Inbred

Temperament: Distilled
Grooming needs: You should oughta try
Exercise needs: He don't need none
Obedience: He don't need no tellin' twice
Ideal Owners: Farmboys

**Spaniel**
Sleepy
Laid back
Mellow

**Why You Should**
He won't mash your buttons

**Why You Shouldn't**
You don't like rye

Do y'all live in Tennessee? And don't you jus' love the good ol' Southern lifestyle? Don't like to do nothin' no faster than the good Lord intended you to? Why, then meet the Jack Spaniel, who's a-fixin' to be your friend, just as soon as he's done gone for his afternoon nap. He like to slept all day once, and that ain't no lie. But he'll most likely wake up when you pour a drink.

## Bulldog
Rude
Flatulent
Butch

# Bull-Shiht

*blah! BLAH! blah! blah! BLAH! BLAH!*

Temperament: Confused
Grooming needs: Constant
Exercise needs: There's no time
Obedience: Flunks everything
Ideal Owners: Confused

## Shih Tzu
Dainty
Frivolous
Decorative

**Why You Should**
You're full of it

**Why You Shouldn't**
Isn't it obvious?

You'd never expect to meet the burly Bulldog and the diminutive Shih Tzu in the same room, let alone the same body. Butch combined with bitch, you can be forgiven for dreading the results. And yet the zen from centuries of palace-and-temple life blends surprisingly well with the Best of British breeding and the Winston Churchill look. *And if you believe that...*

# TOY DOGS

We've all seen the educational materials telling us that "a dog is not a toy," but hey--sometimes a dog seems pretty much just like a toy. So if you want a cutesy little plaything to amuse you, and you prefer low-maintenance in the pet department, and your home is smaller than the White House, check out *these* toys.

## Bichon Frise

Absorbent
Comforting
Bitchy

# Bichweiler

Temperament: High-spending
Grooming needs: High-maintenance
Exercise needs: Savaging the ex
Obedience: Responds to you, ignores him
Ideal Owners: Bitter, discarded wives

## Rottweiler

Threatening
Expensive
Litigious

**Why You Should**
For the bitch-fest

If you're a not-so-gay divorcee and you've been shunned by the ladies who lunch, you need company to help you while away the hours before the divorce settlement comes through. Rack up bills on the

**Why You Shouldn't**
Offputting to new suitors

ex's credit cards until you no longer care about his younger, slimmer model. Your loving Bichweiler will soak up your drunken tears *and* menace your miserable, good-for-nothing ex.

# Cocktese

**Cocker spaniel**
Coquettish
Charming
Scheming

Temperament: Alluring
Grooming needs: Show-stopping
Exercise needs: Tango or can-can
Obedience: Finishing school
Ideal Owners: Eligible girls

**Maltese**
Teasing
Pleasing
Fleecing

**Why You Should**
To attract admirers

Are you a single girl looking to marry well? The Cocktese is small enough to fit in your Hermes holdall and join you at the lunches, benefits and openings that are the hunting grounds for rich men. With her pert good looks, she's sure to melt a man's heart (and wallet). Make sure to pick one that complements your tones, and if not, have your colorist work some magic on you.

**Why You Shouldn't**
She might upstage you

# Toy Box

### Toy fox terrier
Miniature
Fits in a box
Cute

Temperament: Playful
Grooming needs: Barbie brush
Exercise needs: Kiddie pool
Obedience: Put him back in his box
Ideal Owners: Kids (and big kids)

### Boxer
Sporting
Fun
Plays ball

"Mom, can we keep him?" Every parent dreads this moment, but you could be onto a winner with a Toy Box. He'll provide constant entertainment for Junior, but he doesn't take up much space or eat all your food. He doesn't need walking, and even his poops only smell of modeling clay.

**Why You Should**
It'll be fun!

**Why You Shouldn't**
Is it time to grow up?

You might find he brings out the inner kid in you, too.

# French Kiss

**Bichon Frise**
Chic
Gorgeous
Pampered

Temperament: Sense of entitlement
Grooming needs: Strictly Chanel
Exercise needs: *"Pardon?"*
Obedience: Responds to seduction
Ideal Owners: Incurable poseur/romantics

**French bulldog/Keeshond**
A) Perverse
B) Fluffy

**Why You Should**
That *je ne sais quoi*

You love the land of wine, cheese, garlic and Gauloises. You just want life to be beautiful, and where else but Paris do people know how to treat a dog right? Your pooch is welcome in every bistro and carried in every fashionable handbag. This is one totally chic *chien* to be seen with, and he has a deliciously sexy voice, too: *"Weurf, weurf!"*

**Why You Shouldn't**
His oral hygiene

# Bonsai

**Borzoi**
Reserved
Quiet
Likes trees

**Japanese Chin**
Zen
Meditative
Static

Temperament: Wallflower
Grooming needs: Occasional pruning
Exercise needs: Yoga balances
Obedience: Napoleonic
Ideal Owners: Small-apartment dwellers

Like short men, small dogs tend to think they can conquer the world: yap, yap, yap. But when location, location, location and a small paycheck combine, a postage-stamp-sized abode is all you can get. So downsize on the dog front with a pocket-sized pup. He can gambol around his pot when he's watered, and otherwise just hang out looking decorative.

**Why You Shouldn't**
You'll forget to water him

**Why You Should**
What's not to like?

# Shrug

**Shiba Inu**
Coordinated
Snobbish
Vain

**Pug**
Loyal
Devoted
Lazy

Temperament: Cuddlesome
Grooming needs: Dry clean only
Exercise needs: Catwalk
Obedience: zzzzz...
Ideal Owners: Fashion victims

**Why You Should**
You like cuddles

**Why You Shouldn't**
Fur makes you itch

This is the perfect dog to have around when all you want is a hug! Shrugs love nothing more than draping themselves across their owners' shoulders and having a nap. And when you're going out, the Shrug needn't be left home alone. In his favorite position, he makes the perfect scarf to go with any outfit. Just make sure you don't forget to wipe all that drool off your shoulder.

# airehead

**Airedale terrier**
Ditsy
Blonde
Vacant

Temperament: Spacy
Grooming needs: Peroxide
Exercise needs: Batting eyelashes
Obedience: Sure, why not?
Ideal Owners: Valley girls

**A. N. Other**
Mutt
Whatever
Y'know?

Wouldn't it, you know, like, be really like great to have like a dog? Cuz like dogs are way cool and real happy and stuff and you could be real happy and stuff too if you, like, had one too, right? So, y'know, breeds are *so* yesterday, man, so you gotta go, like, *designer*. OK, so maybe it's a mutt, but you can only get it in Airedale, so that's designer, right? So that makes it, like, *way* valuable and stuff.

Why You Should
Like, why not?

Why You Shouldn't
Whatever, dude

89

# Pompadour

**Pomeranian**
Coiffed
Quiffed
yet...Casual

Temperament: Tsssst!...hot!
Grooming needs: Wax, spray & backcombing
Exercise needs: Chasing birds
Obedience: Slave to fashion
Ideal Owners: James Dean & Elvis fans

**Labrador**
Lovable
Popular
Rockabilly

**Why You Should**
You're a 50s freak

If you're approaching your midlife crisis and you've already got the retro sports car, but you're not in a position to get away with a ridiculous haircut, the trendy Pompadour might just be the answer to your follicular frustration. This hound dog is cool: he ain't nothing but a hairdo without a cause. You can take him out hotrodding in your blue suede shoes.

**Why You Shouldn't**
You're 50-something

# Corker

**Corgi**
Dapper
Regal
Inbred

Temperament: Colonel Mustard
Grooming needs: Mrs Peacock
Exercise needs: Billiard room
Obedience: Suspect
Ideal Owners: Miss Scarlet

**Cocker spaniel**
Fiendishly clever
Cunning
Inquisitive

Next time you're invited to a Murder Mystery party, why not take along your Corker and work as a team? He's bound to get the culprit to confess, so let him do the detective work while you devote your sleuthing talents to hunting down Mr/Ms Right. Don't let him sniff you out when you're hiding in the dark with your victim, though!

Why You Should
You haven't got a clue

Why You Shouldn't
It's cheating

# Boxer Chocs

**Boxer**
Expensive
Velvety
Brown

Temperament: Sugar and spice
Grooming needs: Can get sticky
Exercise needs: Laps around the sofa
Obedience: Sycophantic
Ideal Owners: Philanderers' wives

**Chocolate labrador**
Sweet
Smooth
Soft-centered

**Why You Should**
You're in trouble

Don't know what to get your valentine? Came home late with lipstick on your collar and need to make up? Don't insult her with flowers, go for the Boxer Chocolates. While it won't entirely get you off the hook, at least she'll be yelling about who's going to housebreak and walk the boisterous pup, instead of getting at you for your shameful indiscretions.

**Why You Shouldn't**
You'll be in more trouble

# INDEX